CW00544496

MOSES
and the People of God

Contemporary Bible Series
MOSES and the People of God
Retold by Joy Melissa Jensen
Published by
Scandinavia Publishing House 2009
Drejervej 15,3   DK-2400 Copenhagen NV,
Denmark
Tel. (45) 3531 0330 Fax (45) 3536 0334
E-mail: info@scanpublishing.dk
Web: www.scandinavia.dk

Text copyright
© Scandinavia Publishing House
Illustrations copyright © Gustavo Mazali
Design by Ben Alex
Printed in China
ISBN 978 87 7247 484 7

MOSES

and the People of God

Retold for Children

by Joy Melissa Jensen

scandinavia

Contents

Slavery in Egypt

Exodus 1:6-14

Joseph's family lived in the region of Goshen for 400 years. While Joseph was alive, the Hebrews lived in peace. But many years after Joseph had died, a new king ruled over Egypt. This king did not know about all the good things Joseph had done. He wanted the Hebrews out of Egypt. "They have taken over our land," he complained. "Soon they will take

over our people too."

So the king forced the Hebrews to be slaves. They had to work all day whether it was roasting hot or freezing cold. They had to mix cement and carry bricks and build entire cities. It was hard work, and they were not treated very well. But even though the work was miserable, their families grew larger and spread throughout the land. This just made the Egyptians hate them even more.

The King's Order

Exodus 1:15-22

The king called in Shiprah and Puah to see him. They were midwives who helped women give birth to their babies. He told them, "I want you to kill every baby boy among the Hebrews." The midwives were shocked, but they agreed to the king's demand.

When the time came for a Hebrew woman to give birth, the midwives hoped the child would be a girl. But if it was a boy, they still would not kill the child.

The king knew the women had disobeyed his orders. "Didn't you hear me?" he asked them angrily, "I told you to kill all the Hebrew boys!"

The women made up a story. "Your majesty," they told him, "Hebrew women have their babies much quicker than Egyptian women. By the time we arrive, it's already too late to kill them." So the king sent out a command all over Egypt saying, "As soon as a Hebrew boy is born, he must be thrown into the Nile River!"

Moses is Born

Exodus 2:1-4

During this time there was a man and a woman from the tribe of Levi living in Egypt. The woman had just given birth to a baby boy. When she heard the king's order, she panicked. She loved her baby; he was her pride and joy. So she searched her house and found a spot where she could hide him and kept him hidden for three months. During this time the king's officials were roaming the country. They were killing every baby boy that belonged to the Hebrews.

The woman decided she had to find a better hiding spot. So she gathered some long reeds and weaved a basket out of them.

She put her baby in the basket. Then she sneaked down to the riverbank, and she let the basket float among the bulrushes on the water. Miriam, the baby's older sister, had followed her mother down to the river. Her mother went back home. But Miriam stayed crouching down in the grass. She wanted to watch over her brother and see what would happen to him.

Saved by a Princess

Exodus 2:5-10

That evening the king's daughter was heading down toward the river to bathe. As she approached the riverbank, she saw something floating on the water. "Quick, go and fetch that basket!" she called to her servant. The servant waded into the river and carried the basket back to the princess. They were surprised to see a little baby boy inside. His cheeks were rosy from crying. "The poor child," exclaimed the princess. "He must be one of the Hebrew babies." The princess picked up the baby, and she rocked him in her arms until he fell asleep.

Miriam had been watching the whole thing. She went over to the princess and said politely, "Your Majesty, I can see that you love this little baby. Perhaps I could find a woman to care for him until he is old enough for you to keep him."

The princess smiled at Miriam.

"Yes, that's a fine idea," she said. So Miriam took her little brother back to their mother. She raised the boy until he was old enough to be adopted. Then she took him to the princess. "He's yours now," the boy's mother said. "What will you name him?" The princess said, "His name will be Moses."

Moses Stands Up for a Slave

Exodus 2:11-14

Moses grew up in the palace. He had the best of everything. At mealtimes he had plenty to eat. And he wore only the finest clothes. One day Moses took a walk outside of the palace grounds. He saw the Hebrews slaving away under the hot sun. Then he noticed that one of them was being whipped by an Egyptian slave master. Moses was furious and ran over to save the man who was being beaten. He grabbed the slave master with both hands and killed him. Moses tried to hide the body in the sand. But someone found out about what he had done. Everybody began to gossip about Moses. The king was so angry that he sent his men to arrest Moses and have him killed. Moses had to run away. He did not stop until he crossed the border and reached the land of Midian in the desert.

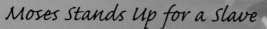

Jethro Welcomes Moses

Exodus 2:14-21

Once Moses arrived in Midian, he was tired and thirsty. He sat down by a well and had a drink of water. Just then, the seven daughters of a priest named Jethro came to the well to give water to their sheep and goats. But a group of shepherds tried to bully them. Moses stood up for the girls and chased the shepherds away. Then Moses offered to water the women's sheep and goats himself. They thanked him and went back to their father's house.

"Why did you take so long?" he asked when they came in. The women told their father about

the shepherds who bullied them. "But a young Hebrew helped us," they explained. "And he even watered our flocks."

"Why didn't you invite him home?" Jethro replied. "We must return his kindness and let him stay with us."

The girls went back to find Moses. They invited him to come and live with them. So Moses stayed with Jethro, and he even married one of his daughters named Zipporah.

15

The Burning Bush

Exodus 3:1-10

One day Moses was guarding Jethro's sheep and goats on the mountainside. He was wandering along the trail when suddenly, something incredible happened. He saw a bush light up in flames. As he stepped closer to get a better look, he noticed that the bush was not burning up. Then the voice of God called to Moses from the bush,

"Moses, I am here to tell you what I plan to do. I have not forgotten my beloved people. I know that they are suffering as slaves in Egypt. They have prayed to me and I will answer their prayers. I have something special in store for them. And I have chosen you, Moses, to lead my people out of Egypt. You will bring them safely to the land I have promised your ancestors. Now go to the king, and ask him to free my people."

Moses Can Perform Miracles

Exodus 3:11-18

Moses was frightened. He hid his face behind his hands. "But why have you chosen me?" he asked God.

"Don't worry Moses," God replied. "I am with you! Throw your walking stick on the ground." Moses obeyed. When the stick hit the ground it turned into a slithering snake at Moses' feet. "Now pick the snake up by the tail," God said. Moses bent down and grabbed the tail. The snake went stiff and turned back into a walking stick.

Then the Lord said, "Now put your hand under your shirt." Moses obeyed. When he pulled his hand out again, it was ghostly white and covered with scales. Moses was scared, so he put his hand under his shirt and took it out again. Now it was normal. God said, "These miracles will show everyone that I have sent you to save my people. If they still do not believe you, take some water from the Nile River. Pour it on the ground, and I will turn the water into blood before their eyes."

19

Aaron and Moses

Exodus 4:14-17, 27-31

"Lord," Moses said, "If I go to the king, he will not listen to me. Besides, I am not a good speaker. I stutter, and I talk too slow."

So the Lord said, "Your brother Aaron is a good speaker. He will speak for you. I will be with both of you and tell you what to say."

So Moses met Aaron on the mountainside. They greeted each other with a kiss. Moses told Aaron everything that God had said. Aaron agreed to go with Moses and see the king. But first they met with the Hebrew leaders.

"The time has come for the Lord to lead his people out of Egypt! And Moses is the man God has chosen to lead them," Aaron told them. The leaders did not believe them. "We've been in slavery for hundreds of years!" they said. "Why would God free us now?"

To show them it was true Moses took his walking stick and threw it on the ground. The men jumped back in surprise when the stick turned into a snake. Then Moses performed the other miracles. The leaders realized that Moses and Aaron were telling the truth. They bowed down on the ground and thanked the Lord for his goodness.

Let My People Go
Exodus 4:19–5:2

Moses and Aaron traveled to Egypt and arrived at the king's palace. They stood before him and said, "God has appeared to us, and he has asked that you let his people go!" But the king barely even looked at Moses and Aaron.

"Why should I obey this God of yours?" he snarled. "Go away." Aaron threw the walking stick on the ground, and it turned into a snake. The king thought they were just playing a trick. He called in his magicians, and they used their secret powers to make snakes out of sticks too. Then Aaron's snake swallowed the other snakes. But the Lord had made the king stubborn.

"You're wasting my time and everyone else's too," he told Moses and Aaron. "Go away! I will not let your people go."

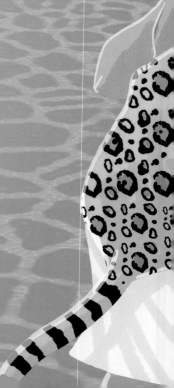

23

Blood and Frogs

Exodus 7:14-24, Exodus 8:1-15

Moses and Aaron felt discouraged. But the Lord came to them and said, "I will bring ten plagues on Egypt, one after the other. These horrible things will not happen to the Hebrews because I will keep them safe."

Then God told Moses and Aaron to take the walking stick and hold it out over the Nile River. They obeyed and watched the water turn into blood. The fish in the water died, and people had to walk around pinching their noses from the awful stink. Not a drop of clean water was left anywhere in Egypt. When the king saw this he began to worry. But he still refused to let the people go.

Now God sent the second plague—frogs. They went hopping and croaking down streets and right into people's homes. Not even the king could get away from them. Frogs jumped on his dinner table and slept on his pillow. "Please," the king begged Moses and Aaron, "I will let your people go, just get rid of these frogs!" Moses prayed and God made all the frogs die. But once the king saw that things were back to normal, he still did not let God's people go.

Gnats and Flies

Exodus 8:16-32

The Lord said to Moses, "Take the walking stick and strike the ground with it. I will turn all the dust into gnats, and they will swarm all over Egypt." Moses obeyed. And the sky became black with little buzzing gnats.

Gnats landed in people's hair and covered the animals.

"What's the big deal?" said the king. "My magicians can turn dust into gnats too." But when the magicians tried, they could not do it.

"God must have done this," they told the king. But the king didn't listen.

26

Then the Lord said to Moses and Aaron, "Go to the king and say, 'The Lord commands you to let his people go.' When he refuses, I will send another plague upon Egypt." They obeyed. But just like God said, the king wouldn't listen. So the Lord sent millions of flies to infest Egypt. People had to swat them away all day long. They could not get any work done, and they couldn't sleep at night. The king begged Moses and Aaron, "I will do whatever you ask, as long as you get these flies out of here!" So Moses prayed, and God took the flies away. But the king was not telling the truth. He still refused to let God's people go.

Disease and Sores

Exodus 9:1-12

The Lord sent Moses to the king again. "If you don't let God's people go," he said, "he will bring an awful disease on all your animals." The king was stubborn. He still would not let the people go.

So the very next day God sent a disease on the Egyptian's animals. Their horses and donkeys, camels and cattle, sheep and goats—all got sick and died. The people could no longer get meat or milk. There were no donkeys or camels to carry heavy loads. And they had no wool to use for warm blankets and clothes.

Next God commanded Moses and Aaron to scoop up ash from

28

the stove. Then he sent them to
the king. Moses threw the ash
into the air, and it turned into a
disease. The Egyptians became
covered with sores. Their skin
was spotted like a leopard, and
they were red and itchy all over.
Even the king's magicians were
too miserable to get out of bed.
But the king still refused to let
God's people go.

29

Hail and Locusts

Exodus 9:13-35, Exodus 10:1-20

Then God told Moses, "Stretch your arms toward the sky. I will send the worst hailstorm in the history of Egypt." So Moses lifted his arms up, and the sky grew dark. Thunder rumbled loudly. Lightning flashed through the black clouds and struck the ground. Then God sent hail. The hailstones fell like heavy rocks—they pounded the earth and flattened the harvests. The king was terrified. He sent for Moses and Aaron and told them, "I will let your people go if you get rid of this hail!" But after God stopped the hailstorm, the king still didn't keep his promise.

"How much longer are you going to disobey the Lord?" Aaron asked the king. "Your people are suffering. Your animals have died. Your country is a disaster."

"All right, all right," said the king, "you can go, but only the men." Moses and Aaron refused the king's offer. They knew that God wanted all of them to leave Egypt, not just some of them. So the Lord sent a wind full of locusts. They ate everything, and there was not a single flower or green plant left in Egypt. The king still refused to let the people go.

Darkness and Death

Exodus 10:21-29, Exodus 11:1-10

Now the Lord told Moses, "Stretch your arms up to the sky. I will cover Egypt with darkness thick enough to touch." Moses obeyed, and blackness covered everything. No one could see anything at all. The people stayed inside their homes and did not come out for three days. The king called Moses and Aaron to him and said, "All right! You may go, but you must leave your animals behind."

"No," Moses said. "We will all go together, even the animals."

Then the Lord said to Moses, "I will send one last punishment on the king of Egypt and his people. This time the king will not only let you leave, he'll chase you out."

Moses went to the king and said, "The Lord has asked you to let his people go, and you have refused. Tonight he will pass over Egypt. Everywhere he goes, the firstborn son in every Egyptian family will die. No family will be left out, including your own son. When this happens, you will know it, because there will be so much crying that you will have to cover your ears. But the Hebrews will have no reason to cry. You will know that the Lord is with his people, and you will let us go."

God Keeps His Promise

Exodus 12:1-41

The Lord told Moses and Aaron to speak to his people. They told them, "The time has come for the Lord to lead our families out of Egypt! He has asked you to celebrate with a special Passover meal. Cook a young lamb and eat it with bitter herbs and bread. After you have finished eating, put some blood from the lamb on the doorposts. Have sandals on your feet and walking sticks in your hands. There will be a long journey ahead."

The people did everything God told them to do. During the

34

night God passed over the houses of the Egyptians, and every firstborn son died. But he spared the houses that had blood on the doorposts.

Before dawn, the whole country was crying for their lost family members. The king's son died too. He called for Moses and Aaron. "Get out of here," he told them, "and never come back!"

Everything happened just as God had said. Finally the Hebrews were free! Moses called all the people together and they finally left.

The Exodus

Exodus 13:17-22

God led his people through the deserts of Egypt. He never left them. During the day he appeared as a cloud leading the way before them. At night, he lit up their path in the form of a flaming light. The people walked a long way, and when they came to a place called Etham near the border, they needed a rest.

They set up camp, but God told them to turn back and camp in a different spot. He wanted the king and his army to chase after Israel. He was going to show his great power and help the Israelites win. The people obeyed, and camped where God led them. Then they pitched their tents, tied up their animals and went to sleep.

37

The King's Chase

Exodus 14:1-14

The king of Egypt got the news that the Hebrews were leaving his country. "Look what we've done!" he shouted to his men. "We let them go and now we'll have no slaves." He had already forgotten about the plagues the Lord had sent on the Egyptian people. Every horse-drawn chariot was loaded with soldiers. The king led them on a chase to capture the people of Israel.

Finally they caught up with them at their camp. When the Hebrews saw the chariots heading towards them, they were frightened and ran to Moses. "You brought us out of slavery only to die here in the desert," they moaned, "and now the king will kill us all!" But Moses knew that the Lord had a plan. "Don't be afraid," he said. "You will see God work his miracles. Have faith! God will take care of us."

The Parting of the Red Sea

Exodus 14:15-31

God told Moses, "Tell the people to start heading toward the Red Sea. When you get to the water, hold your walking stick out. I will part the waters and you will be able to march across to the other side." So Moses led the people toward the sea. As they approached the shore, Moses held his walking stick out. The waters began to part straight down the middle and build up like two mighty walls on either side. Israel crossed over the Red Sea. The Egyptian army was amazed. They followed right behind in their chariots.

Once Moses reached the other side, he waited until all the people had safely crossed over. Then he held out his walking stick above the water, and the waves crashed together again. The Egyptian army drowned with their chariots in the wild, foamy waves.

Water for the Thirsty

Exodus 15:1-27

The Israelites celebrated their victory. The Lord had saved them! They sang out, "Praise the Lord for his great victory! He has thrown the horses and their riders into the sea." Moses' sister Miriam shook her tambourine and began to dance and sing. The other women joined in and praised the Lord with their songs.

After many hours of rejoicing, Moses led the people into the Shur Desert. They walked for three days without water. The people were tired and thirsty. Finally they found some water at a place called Marah. But as soon as they took a drink, they spit it out again. The water tasted bitter and had a horrible aftertaste. "What are we going to drink?" they asked Moses. But Moses didn't know, so he prayed. God told Moses to throw a piece of wood into the water. Moses obeyed, and the water turned clean and fresh. The people drank as much as they could. Then they filled up their casks and walked on.

That evening, they came to an oasis with twelve springs and seventy palm trees. They stopped there and camped for the night.

Food for the Hungry

Exodus 15:1-16:20

The people walked through the desert a long time. They were heading toward Mount Sinai across the western edge of the desert. The sun beat down on them, and they were running out of food. "It's a shame we're not slaves in Egypt anymore," they began to complain. "At least we had bread and meat and a chance to sit down. Out here we'll starve!"

God spoke to Moses and said, "I have heard my people's cry. Tell them I will send food from heaven. Then they will know I am God, and they will trust in me."

That evening a flock of quail landed in the campsite among their tents. The people roasted the birds and ate the delicious meat. Then they went to sleep. The next morning they woke up to a sound like falling rain. When they peeked out of their tents, they saw the ground was covered with little white flakes. "What is this?" they asked each other. Moses answered, "This is the bread God has given us to eat today." The people called the bread Manna. It tasted like sweet wafers made with honey. The people gathered up the Manna bread and ate till they were full.

The People Doubt God
Exodus 17:1-7

The Lord led the people, and they traveled onward. But their water supply had already run out, and they were getting thirsty again. "We need something to drink," the people complained to Moses. "Do you want us to die of thirst?" Moses didn't know when they would find water again. He bowed his head in prayer. "Forgive the people, Lord. They are impatient. But it's true, they do need water."

God told Moses, "When you get to the rock at the foot of Mount Sinai, hit it with your walking stick. I will make water pour out of it."

Moses trusted God and led the people to the rock. But the people were still complaining bitterly, saying, "Is God really with us? Is Moses telling us the truth when he says God will bring us water?" Finally they reached the rock. Moses struck it with his stick, and just as God had promised, water poured out. They drank it and felt strong again. But they still doubted God. So Moses named that place Massah, which means "testing," and Meribah, which means "complaining."

46

At The Foot of Mount Sinai

Exodus 19:1-18

Two months had passed since the people of Israel left Egypt. The people camped at the foot of Mount Sinai. Moses went up to the top to pray to God. God told Moses, "I have cared for you just like a mighty eagle cares for his young. If you continue to obey me, Israel will be my holy nation. Go and tell the people this good news."

So Moses went back down the mountain. He told the people what God had said, and the people promised to love and

48

obey the Lord. They stayed at the camp three more days and celebrated God's goodness. But on the third day they woke up to storm clouds. There was thunder and lightning, and black smoke covered the top of Mount Sinai. Then the people heard the sound of a horn blast.

Moses called the people together and he took them to the foot of the mountain. They looked up and saw a fire on top of the mountain. Then God told Moses to climb the mountain and meet him there.

49

The Ten Commandments

Exodus 20:1-17

When Moses reached the top, God spoke to him from the blazing fire. "I am God, the one who has brought you out of slavery in Egypt," he said. "These are my Ten Commandments:

Do not worship any God but me.

Do not worship idols and false images.

Do not swear and misuse my name.

Remember the seventh day— the Sabbath, and keep it holy.

Respect your father and mother.

Do not murder.

Be faithful in marriage.
Do not steal.
Do not tell lies about others.
Do not want anything that belongs to someone else."

When God had finished speaking to Moses, he gave him two stone tablets with the Ten Commandments carved into them.

God's Promises for Israel

Exodus 23:20-33

God said to Moses, "I will send an angel ahead of you on your journey. The angel will bring you to the land I have prepared for your people. There are people already living in this land. But these people worship false gods, and they will try to get you to worship their gods. Don't make any agreements with them. You must remain faithful to me. If you do, I will bless your land. Your valleys will flow with milk and honey; your fruit will grow plump and sweet; your

crops will always be plentiful. I will take away sickness among your people. New babies will be born and people will live happy lives into old age." These are the things God promised Moses and the people of Israel.

The People Agree to Obey God

Exodus 24:4-11

Moses wrote down everything the Lord told him. He was eager to tell the people of Israel. But first he wanted to build an altar to worship God. He woke up early the next morning and set up twelve large stones, one for each of the twelve tribes. Then he burned special offerings and sacrificed a few bulls. Finally he called all the people together. He read to them aloud from the Lord's Ten Commandments. When he finished, the people shouted, "We will obey the Lord!"

Moses took some of the blood from the sacrifices and sprinkled it on the people. "With this blood the Lord makes his agreement with you," he told them. Then Moses and Aaron went up to the mountain together with some of the leaders. God met them on the mountain. Under his feet was something like a jewel blue pavement, bright as the sun. The leaders of Israel were amazed. They thought that if you saw God, you would die. But they didn't die, so they stayed on the mountain and ate and drank.

The Golden Calf

Exodus 32:1-14

While Moses was on the mountaintop, the people down below began to feel restless. "Why is Moses taking so long?" they complained. "He may as well have died up there!" The people went to Aaron and said to him, "We need a god to worship. We can't wait any longer for Moses." So Aaron asked the people to give him all their gold jewelry. Then Aaron melted the jewelry down and molded it into a golden calf. The people began to worship the calf as a god. "This is the god that brought us out of Egypt!" they cheered as they danced around the golden calf and bowed down before it. Then they ate and drank and celebrated their new god.

The Lord saw all of this, and he was angry. "Go and see what the people are doing!" he said to Moses. "They are already disobeying me. I'm angry enough to destroy them!"

Moses pleaded, "Please God, don't harm them. Otherwise the Egyptians will laugh and say you saved us just to destroy us."

Moses Destroys the Idol

Exodus 32:14-20

Moses ran back down the mountain still holding the Ten Commandments. Finally he came to the foot of Mount

58

Sinai where his people were dancing around the statue of a golden calf and worshiping it. "Why are you worshiping a dead statue?" Moses shouted. "The one true God is with you. Have you forgotten him already?"

Moses was so angry, he threw the stone tablets on the ground, and they shattered into little pieces. Then Moses marched over to the golden calf and ground it up into dust. He threw the dust into the people's drinking water. Then Moses ordered the people to drink it. He did not want any trace left of the false idol.

That night Moses prayed for the people. He asked God to forgive their sins. God listened to Moses and he promised to stay with the people of Israel.

God Shows Mercy

Exodus 33:12-35

Moses prayed to the Lord, "You have chosen me to lead your people. But I still don't know who will help me. Let me know your plans. Then I can obey you. Remember you have chosen the nation of Israel to be your people."

The Lord replied, "Be at peace. I will go with you."

Moses said, "If you go with us, everyone will know that you love your people. Everyone will say that the nation of Israel is blessed."

The Lord told him, "You've made me happy. And you've always obeyed me. Because I am your friend, I will do just as you have asked."

Moses said, "Lord, since you are pleased with me, let me see you!"

The Lord answered, "You cannot see my face. But I will hide you in the rock's cleft and put my hand over your eyes. Once I pass by, I will take my hand away. You will see my back. And my glory will pass over you."

After forty days and forty nights on the mountain Moses finally returned to the people with two new stone tablets. The people were amazed and dared not go close to him. His face was shining with the glory of God.

The Contemporary Bible Series